HABITANT POEMS

NEW CANADIAN LIBRARY NO. 11

HABITANT

MCCLELLAND AND STEWART LIMITED

William Henry Drummond

POEMS

Introduction & selection: Arthur L. Phelps

General Editor: Malcolm Ross

The Canadian Publishers
McClelland and Stewart Limited
25 Hollinger Road, Toronto

0-7710-9111-7

PRINTED AND BOUND IN CANADA BY
T. H. BEST PRINTING COMPANY LIMITED

Contents

Introduction

I remember when a country parson at a concert after a fall fowl supper would recite "The Wreck of the *Julie Plante*," and then, as encore, "De Nice Leetle Canadienne" to pokes and smirks and thumping applause. Afterwards, the established literati of the community, to maintain their repute, would toss off with cunning nonchalance the word "habitant" with the "h" buried and the last "t" nearly gone. The French were amusing and could even be talked about. W. H. Drummond's verses were doing a job.

William Henry Drummond was born in Ireland in 1854. With his mother, father, and three brothers he came to Canada before he was eleven years old. A few months after the family's arrival in Canada the father died and the mother faced life in the new world with four boys about her, the oldest of whom was young William Henry. The family struggle, with a competent woman handling it, was but duplication of thousands of such in the new country. Young William became an expert telegrapher at fifteen and was stationed at Bord à Plouffe on the Rivière des Prairies not far from Montreal. The late J. F. Macdonald of Queen's, who wrote of Drummond with delighted understanding, saw thus the poet in the making:

> The little village was a centre for the lumber trade, especially the rafting. Here young Drummond first came to know the French Canadian habitant and voyageur. At least one poem, "The Wreck of the *Julie Plante*," is directly due to his acquaintance with an old lumberman of the village, Gidéon Plouffe, whose description of a storm, "an' de win' she blow, blow, blow," rang in Drummond's ears till he wrote the poem with these words setting the tune.

The boy with the west coast of Ireland and its banshee and leprechaun legends inside him, became the youth listening to the tales of the Quebec river-drivers and farmers. The Montreal High School, McGill University, and Bishop's College at Lennoxville, gave the developing man his education and professional training. He practised medicine in the Eastern Townships and in Montreal. In 1907 he died suddenly in the Cobalt mining country. The younger brothers had mining interests there and William Henry had gone up from Montreal to fight an outbreak of smallpox in the camps. At fifty-three Dr.

Drummond had lived ardently and variously as physician, fisherman, tramper of snow-shoe and toboggan trails, and gay companion. He was also an apt and easy versifier and, at the centre of all his interests and activities, a poet.

It has been suggested that Drummond used the French-Canadian "broken" English in its narrative and dramatic form as an invention behind which a shyness about his warmest and finest feelings might hide itself. There is another view. Drummond did not invent the kind of expression he used; he heard it all about him. And he was not so much shy about himself as, frankly and openly, delighted with others. He revelled in his subjects and forgot himself. In the French-Canadian pieces, where he was most at home with his material, he was most fully the artist. Whether he himself really knew it or not, his job as artist lay in his depiction of an aspect of French-Canadian life passing before his eyes and sounding richly in his ears. That depiction, because the commitment to it was warm and intimate and thorough, marked some of Drummond's work for currency beyond his own place and time.

At this distance in time critical risks are involved in the attempt to characterize and assess the nature of the Drummond contribution. In 1897, as an Introduction to a collection of Drummond's pieces, Louis Fréchette, whom Drummond called the Poet Laureate, exchanged acknowledgements by characterizing Drummond as "the pathfinder of a new land of song." Originally, the phrase had been applied to Fréchette himself by Longfellow. Fréchette passes it on, as he says, "Avec mille fois plus de raison." It was a cordial and a gracious time. The whole of Drummond's defence of his work (and he anticipated the need for such defence), and the reply to the fad which in our day deplores his "bastard diction," lies in one sentence in his preface to that 1897 collection:

> I have endeavoured to paint a few types, and in doing this, it has seemed to me that I could best attain the object in view by having my friends tell their own tales in their own way, as they would relate them to English-speaking auditors not conversant with the French tongue.

"My friends tell their own tales . . . as they would relate them to English-speaking auditors not conversant with the French tongue." In those phrases is Drummond's mandate, and he was sufficiently self-analytic and sufficiently secure in his sense of his own achievement to know it.

But the Drummond vogue is dead. No fowl supper crowds today slap their thighs and pound the floor to his rhythms and his warm and loving fun. English-speaking Canadians no longer heed nor think they need Drummond's interpretations of Quebec. French-speaking Canadians tend to offer him even less than the tribute of critical disdain. There is no parallel today for the fraternity of Louis Fréchette.

Yet Drummond persists. One must ask why.

Again, to go back into that other century is to find an answer. Neil Monroe (who knows anything of Neil Monroe today!) in his critical sketch of Drummond in 1897 says the habitants of that day were themselves fond of Drummond; they liked him because he liked them. Monroe says:

> They found not only a scrupulous representation of their racial life, customs and character, but the attitude of a sympathetic and admiring friend. A man of the tenderest sentiment, of the finest tact, devoid of any cankering note of superiority, he never wrote a line but in affection, and the humour, wit and pathos of his verses carried the irresistible conviction of a great and generous soul. Of ridicule he was temperamentally incapable; on the human weaknesses of his characters he held his judgement in suspense; he gave to Anglo-Saxon Canadians a new respect for their French compatriots.

How remote it all sounds. How innocent and how refreshing. How far removed from the worlds of the English poets writing in Quebec today, from the insistent incisiveness, the conscience for realistic inclusiveness, of the Scotts, the Dudeks, the Laytons, even of the Kleins. "For the good are always the merry," sang Yeats, and Drummond's time was a merry time.

Drummond belongs to a time and a place. He is rooted in the late nineteenth and the earliest twentieth centuries in Canada, and within Canada, in Quebec, and within Quebec, in a single stratum of her society. The authoritative material for his art, the vitality and insistence in that material which stripped his best writing to clarity and simple order, lay all about him in Quebec. His temperament, warm in humour, rich in philosophic pathos, accorded naturally and sweetly with the lives and ways of his habitant fellow-men. He heard those men and women talk. He watched them live; enjoyed their gaiety; understood their troubles. He loved them. And his verse-making aptitude, set going to record them, found its imperative sanction from them and on their behalf. His Irish and his English verse is merely verse and for the most part ordinary and flaccid; his French-Canadian work moves constantly into poetry. It is the old, old secret of art's accomplishment; Drummond was working in a material he loved and understood. The resultant achievement is a minor one, both in quantity and scope. But it is an achievement within the

tradition of Chaucer, Burns, and Wordsworth,
a branch in a noble tree; and its core is sound.

This means that Drummond today is discard
material only among the undiscerning.

Perhaps the argument should be spelled out. In
"Leetle Bateese" an old French-Canadian
grandpère is talking, addressing the busy, muscular,
mischievous grandson. Every reference, every
picture, every bit of observation and analysis, is
right. The daily ways of the farm are brought alive.
The setting is simply the elemental ordinary
patterns within which a life is lived. The boy is
coming up into those patterns to adjust and accept
and mature. The old man is passing out of the
patterns to know them no more. Drummond's last
stanza carries no lapse from homely immediacy. It
simply rises into comment on universal experience:

> But leetle Bateese! please don't forget
> We rader you're stayin' de small boy yet,
> So chase de chicken an' mak' dem scare
> An' do w'at you lak' wit' your ole gran'père
> For w'en you're beeg feller he won't be dere –
> Leetle Bateese!

In "Philorum's Canoe," the portages, the rapids
and their rocks, the storms and the moonlit nights
are all there. Together the old canoe and the old
man have known them all, and in the end, so
inwoven are the experiences, the canoe's voice is
the man's voice:

> Don't do any good fix me up again, no matter
>   how moche you try,
> For w'en we come ole an' our work she's done
>   bot' man an' canoe mus' die.

"The Wreck of the *Julie Plante*" has the succinct
grimness and tidy economy of many an older ballad.
Generations of fatefulness for the river-driver can
be summed up in,

> For de win' she blow lak' hurricane
>   Bimeby she blow some more . . .

And even when Drummond adds his "Moral,"
compassed in the last stanza, which is advice to the
river-driver to stay home, the humour lies in his
own and the river-driver's knowledge that it is
foolish advice, and no armour against fate:

> Now all good wood scow sailor man
>   Tak' warning by dat storm
> An' go an' marry some nice French girl
>   An' leev on wan beeg farm,
> De win' can blow lak' hurricane
>   An' s'pose she blow some more,
> You can't get drown on Lac St. Pierre
>   So long you stay on shore.

Again, in "The Last Portage," Drummond is
local in detail and universal in reference. There is
"slippery log lyin' ev'ryw'ere": no moon nor star;
"black bush aroun' on de right an' lef'"; "a step
from de road an' you los' you'se'f." But ahead on
the last portage, "is dat leetle boy dancin' dere /

Can see hees w'ite dress an' curly hair" – his long
dead little son.

> An' I foller it on, an' wance in a w'ile
> He turn again wit' de baby smile,
> An' say, "Dear fader, I'm here you see –
> We're bot' togeder, jus' you an' me –
> Very dark to you, but to me it's light,
> De road we travel so far tonight.

In the last two lines of the poem fantasy and reality
the factual immediate and the mysterious, are
interwoven with saving shrewdness.
Characterization is not blurred:

> Was it a dream I dream las' night
> Is goin' away on de morning light?

Drummond's verse in its day was popular verse.
That is, it had a public among people who loved
concerts and recitations. That public heard its own
laughter, enjoyed private jokes and intimate easy
horseplay. It was modest, uninformed, a bit rough
and ready, quite merrily the victim of medicine
man, hypnotist, and pulpit or platform
spell-binder. It was a public which incorporated but
did not dissolve its individuals, in some essentials
unlike the public of today fused under mass media
into mass apathy. This was the public which
enjoyed Drummond.

A selection of Drummond's work in small
compass should be more than merely a pleasant
reminder for the nostalgic. Possessed of some of the

embedded virility which is in all popular verse, these verses may be both rebuke and challenge at a time when Canadian verse-making has become a bit sick with sophistication and has substituted paraded analysis for the self-forgetfulness of spontaneous song.

Yet today there is a difficulty in any attempt to return to an appreciation of Drummond's achievement. The day of groups, and even of crowds, listening with happy communal hilarity to "pieces" being recited seems gone. With it, an opportunity and a function for the Drummond art seems gone. A popular revival of Drummond might come about should some sympathetic and accomplished voice carry his work to the modern microphone. We might then find ourselves assured of three things concerning William Henry Drummond: He possessed what Gregory Clark put his finger on one day at an Ontario Weekly Newspapers Association Convention as the basic sustaining element in Canadian rural life, good humour – "not just humour," Gregory Clark said, "but good humour." And he could tell a story. And he understood the richness and variety and beauty in simple people, who, in any age, are the salt of the earth.

ARTHUR L. PHELPS
THE OLD MILL,
CHAFFEY'S LOCKS

HABITANT POEMS

Leetle Bateese

You bad leetle boy, not moche you care
How busy you 're kipin' your poor gran'père
Tryin' to stop you ev'ry day
Chasin' de hen aroun' de hay—
W'y don't you geev' dem a chance to lay?
                                        Leetle Bateese!

Off on de fiel' you foller de plough
Den we'n you're tire you scare de cow
Sickin' de dog till dey jomp de wall
So de milk ain't good for not'ing at all—
An' you 're only five an' a half dis fall,
                                        Leetle Bateese!

Too sleepy for sayin' de prayer tonight?
Never min' I s'pose it 'll be all right
Say dem tomorrow—ah! dere he go!
Fas' asleep in a minute or so—
An' he 'll stay lak' dat till de rooster crow,
                                        Leetle Bateese!

Den wake us up right away toute suite
Lookin' for somet'ing more to eat,
Makin' me t'ink of dem long leg crane
Soon as dey swaller, dey start again,
I wonder your stomach don't get no pain,
                              Leetle Bateese!

But see heem now lyin' dere in bed,
Look at de arm onderneat' hees head;
If he grow lak' dat till he's twenty year
I bet he 'll be stronger dan Louis Cyr
An' beat all de voyageurs leevin' here,
                              Leetle Bateese!

Jus' feel de muscle along hees back,
Won't geev' heem moche bodder for carry pack
On de long portage, any size canoe,
Dere 's not many t'ing dat boy won't do
For he 's got double-joint on hees body too,
                              Leetle Bateese!

But leetle Bateese! please don't forget
We rader you 're stayin' de small boy yet,
So chase de chicken an' mak' dem scare
An' do w'at you lak' wit' your ole gran'père
For w'en you 're beeg feller he won't be dere—
                              Leetle Bateese!

De Nice Leetle Canadienne

You can pass on de worl' w'erever you lak',
    Tak' de steamboat for go Angleterre,
Tak' car on de State, an' den you come back,
    An' go all de place, I don't care—
Ma frien' dat's a fack, I know you will say,
    W'en you come on dis contree again,
Dere's no girl can touch, w'at we see ev'ry day,
        De nice leetle Canadienne.

Don't matter how poor dat girl she may be,
    Her dress is so neat an' so clean,
Mos' ev'rywan t'ink it was mak' on Paree
    An' she wear it, wall! jus' lak' de Queen.
Den come for fin' out she is mak' it herse'f,
    For she ain't got moche monee for spen',
But all de sam' tam', she was never get lef',
        Dat nice leetle Canadienne.

W'en "un vrai Canayen" is mak' it mariée,
    You t'ink he go leev on beeg flat
An' bodder hese'f all de tam', night an' day,
    Wit' housemaid, an' cook, an' all dat?
Not moche, ma dear frien', he tak' de maison,
    Cos' only nine dollar or ten,
W'ere he leev lak' blood rooster, an' save de l'argent,
    Wit' hees nice leetle Canadienne.

I marry ma famme w'en I 'm jus' twenty year,
    An' now we got fine familee,
Dat skip roun' de place lak' leetle small deer,
    No smarter crowd you never see—
An' I t'ink as I watch dem all chasin' about,
    Four boy an' six girl, she mak' ten,
Dat 's help mebbe kip it, de stock from run out
    Of de nice leetle Canadienne.

O she 's quick an' she 's smart, an' got plaintee heart,
    If you know correc' way go about,
An' if you don't know, she soon tole you so
    Den tak' de firs' chance an' get out;
But if she love you, I spik it for true,
    She will mak' it more beautiful den,
An' sun on de sky can't shine lak' de eye
    Of dat nice leetle Canadienne.

The Wreck of the "Julie Plante"

A LEGEND OF LAC ST. PIERRE

On wan dark night on Lac St. Pierre,
    De win' she blow, blow, blow,
An' de crew of de wood scow "Julie Plante"
    Got scar't an' run below—
For de win' she blow lak' hurricane
    Bimeby she blow some more,
An' de scow bus' up on Lac St. Pierre
    Wan arpent from de shore.

De captinne walk on de fronte deck,
    An' walk de hin' deck too—
He call de crew from up de hole
    He call de cook also.
De cook she 's name was Rosie,
    She come from Montreal,
Was chambre maid on lumber barge,
    On de Grande Lachine Canal.

De win' she blow from nor'-eas'-wes',—
    De sout' win' she blow too,
W'en Rosie cry "Mon cher captinne,
    Mon cher, w'at I shall do?"
Den de captinne t'row de big ankerre,
    But still the scow she dreef',
De crew he can't pass on de shore,
    Becos' he los' hees skeef.

De night was dark lak' wan black cat,
    De wave run high an' fas',
W'en de captinne tak' de Rosie girl
    An' tie her to de mas'.
Den he also tak' de life preserve,
    An' jomp off on de lak',
An' say, "Good-bye, ma Rosie dear,
    I go drown for your sak'."

Nex' morning very early
    'Bout ha'f pas' two—t'ree—four—
De captinne—scow—an' de poor Rosie
    Was corpses on de shore,
For de win' she blow lak' hurricane
    Bimeby she blow some more,
An' de scow bus' up on Lac St. Pierre,
    Wan arpent from de shore.

MORAL

Now all good wood scow sailor man
    Tak' warning by dat storm
An' go an' marry some nice French girl
    An' leev on wan beeg farm.
De win' can blow lak' hurricane
    An' s'pose she blow some more,
You can't get drown on Lac St. Pierre
    So long you stay on shore.

The Voyageur

Dere 's somet'ing stirrin' ma blood tonight,
    On de night of de young new year,
W'ile de camp is warm an' de fire is bright,
    An' de bottle is close at han'—
Out on de reever de nort' win' blow,
Down on de valley is pile de snow,
But w'at do we care so long we know
    We 're safe on de log cabane?

Drink to de healt' of your wife an' girl,
    Anoder wan for your frien',
Den geev' me a chance, for on all de worl'
    I've not many frien' to spare—
I'm born w'ere de mountain scrape de sky,
An' bone of ma fader an' moder lie,
So I fill de glass an' I raise it high
    An' drink to de Voyageur.

For dis is de night of de jour de l 'an,*
    W'en de man of de Grand Nor' Wes'
T'ink of hees home on de St. Laurent,
    An' frien' he may never see—
Gone he is now, an' de beeg canoe
No more you 'll see wit' de red shirt crew,
But long as he leev' he was alway true,
    So we 'll drink to hees memory.

Ax heem de nort' win' w'at he see
    Of de Voyageur long ago,
An' he 'll say to you w'at he say to me,
    So lissen hees story well—
"I see de track of hees botte sau vage†
On many a hill an' long portage
Far, far away from hees own vill age
    An' soun' of de parish bell—

"I never can play on de Hudson Bay
    Or mountain dat lie between
But I meet heem singin' hees lonely way
    De happies' man I know—
I cool hees face as he 's sleepin' dere
Under de star of de Red Rivière,
An' off on de home of de great w'ite bear,
    I 'm seein' hees dog traineau.‡

* *New Year's Day.*   † *Indian boot.*   ‡ *Dog sleigh.*

"De woman an' chil'ren's runnin' out
　　On de wigwam of de Cree—
De leetle papoose dey laugh an' shout
　　W'en de soun' of hees voice dey hear—
De oldes' warrior of de Sioux
Kill hese'f dancin' de w'ole night t'roo,
An de Blackfoot girl remember too
　　De ole tam' Voyageur.

"De blaze of hees camp on de snow I see,
　　An' I lissen hees 'En Roulant'
On de lan' w'ere de reindeer travel free,
　　Ringin' out strong an' clear—
Offen de grey wolf sit before
De light is come from hees open door,
An' caribou foller along de shore
　　De song of de Voyageur.

"If he only kip goin', de red ceinture,*
　　I'd see it upon de Pole
Some mornin' I'm startin' upon de tour
　　For blowin' de worl' aroun'—
But w'erever he sail an' w'erever he ride,
De trail is long an' de trail is wide,
An' city an' town on ev'ry side
　　Can tell of hees campin' groun'."

* Sash worn by the voyageur.

So dat 's de reason I drink tonight
    To de man of de Grand Nor' Wes',
For hees heart was young, an' hees heart was light
    So long as he 's leevin' dere—
I 'm proud of de sam' blood in my vein
I 'm a son of de Nort' Win' wance again
So we 'll fill her up till de bottle 's drain
    An' drink to de Voyageur.

The Last Portage

I'm sleepin' las' night w'en I dream a dream
An' a wonderful wan it seem—
For I' m off on de road I was never see,
Too long an' hard for a man lak' me,
So ole he can only wait de call
Is sooner or later come to all.

De night is dark an' de portage dere
Got plaintee o' log lyin' ev'ryw'ere,
Black bush aroun' on de right an' lef',
A step from de road an' you los' you'se'f
De moon an' de star above is gone,
Yet somet'ing tell me I mus' go on.

An' off in front of me as I go,
Light as a dreef' of de fallin' snow—
Who is dat leetle boy dancin' dere
Can see hees w'ite dress an' curly hair,
An' almos' touch heem, so near to me
In an' out dere among de tree?

An' den I 'm hearin' a voice is say,
"Come along, fader, don't min' de way,
De boss on de camp he sen' for you,
So your leetle boy 's going to guide you t'roo
It 's easy for me, for de road I know,
'Cos I travel it many long year ago."

An' oh! mon Dieu! w'en he turn hees head
I 'm seein' de face of ma boy is dead—
Dead wit' de young blood in hees vein—
An' dere he 's comin' wance more again
Wit' de curly hair, an' dark blue eye,
So lak' de blue of de summer sky—

An' now no more for de road I care,
An' slippery log lyin' ev'ryw'ere—
De swamp on de valley, de mountain too,
But climb it jus' as I use to do—
Don't stop on de road, for I need no res'
So long as I see de leetle w'ite dress.

An' I foller it on, an' wance in a w'ile
He turn again wit' de baby smile,
An' say, "Dear fader, I'm here you see—
We're bot' togeder, jus' you an' me—
Very dark to you, but to me it's light,
De road we travel so far tonight.

"De boss on de camp w'ere I alway stay
Since ever de tam' I was go away,
He welcome de poores' man dat call,
But love de leetle wan bes' of all,
So dat's de reason I spik for you
An' come tonight for to bring you t'roo."

Lak de young Jesu w'en he's here below
De face of ma leetle son look jus' so—
Den off beyon', on de bush I see
De w'ite dress fadin' among de tree—
Was it a dream I dream las' night
Is goin' away on de morning light?

The Habitant

De place I get born, me, is up on de reever
　　Near foot of de rapide dat 's call Cheval Blanc
Beeg mountain behin' it, so high you can't climb it
　　An' whole place she's mebbe two honder' arpent.*

De fader of me, he was habitant farmer,
　　Ma gran' fader too, an' hees fader also,
Dey don't mak' no monee, but dat is n't fonny
　　For it 's not easy get ev'ryt'ing, you mus' know—

All de sam' dere is somet'ing dey got ev'ryboddy,
　　Dat 's plaintee good healt', wat de monee
　　　　can't geev,
So I 'm workin' away dere, an' happy for stay dere
　　On farm by de reever, so long I was leev.

O! dat was de place w'en de spring tam' she's comin',
　　W'en snow go away, an 'de sky is all blue—
W'en ice lef ' de water, an 'sun is get hotter
　　An' back on de medder is sing de gouglou†—

* Acre. † Bobolink.

33

W'en small sheep is firs' comin' out on de pasture,
  Deir nice leetle tail stickin' up on deir back,
Dey ronne wit' deir moder, an' play wit' each oder
  An' jomp all de tam' jus' de sam' dey was crack—

An' ole cow also, she's glad winter is over,
  So she kick herse'f up, an' start off on de race
Wit' de two-year-ole heifer, dat's purty soon lef' her,
  W'y ev'ryt'ing's crazee all over de place!

An' down on de reever de wil' duck is quackin'
  Along by de shore leetle san'piper ronne—
De bullfrog he's gr-rompin' an' doré is jompin'
  Dey all got deir own way for mak' it de fonne.

But spring's in beeg hurry, an' don't stay long wit' us
  An' firs' t'ing we know, she go off till nex' year,
Den bee commence hummin', for summer is comin'
  An' purty soon corn's gettin' ripe on de ear.

Dat's very nice tam' for wake up on de morning
  An' lissen de rossignol sing ev'ry place,
Feel sout' win' a-blowin', see clover a-growin',
  An' all de worl' laughin' itself on de face

Mos' ev'ry day raf' it is pass on de rapide
    De voyageurs singin' some ole chanson
'Bout girl down de reever—too bad dey mus' leave her,
But comin' back soon wit' beaucoup d'argent.

An' den w'en de fall an' de winter come roun' us
    An' bird of de summer is all fly away,
W'en mebbe she's snowin' an' nort' win' is blowin
An' night is mos' t'ree tam' so long as de day.

You t'ink it was bodder de habitant farmer?
    Not at all—he is happy an' feel satisfy,
An' cole may las' good w'ile, so long as de wood-pile
    Is ready for burn on de stove by an' bye.

W'en I got plaintee hay put away on de stable
    So de sheep an' de cow, dey got no chance
        to freeze,
An' de hen all togedder—I don't min' de wedder—
    De nort' win' may blow jus' so moche as she
        please.

An' some cole winter night how I wish you can see us,
    W'en I smoke on de pipe, an' de ole woman sew
By de stove of T'ree Reever—ma wife's fader geev her
    On day we get marry, dat's long tam' ago—

De boy an' de girl, dey was readin' it's lesson,
　　De cat on de corner she's bite heem de pup,
Ole "Carleau" he's snorin' an' beeg stove is roarin'
　　So loud dat I'm scare purty soon she bus' up.

Philomène—dat's de oldes'—is sit on de winder
　　An' kip jus' so quiet lak' wan leetle mouse,
She say de more finer moon never was shiner—
　　Very fonny, for moon is n't dat side de house.

But purty soon den, we hear foot on de outside,
　　An' some wan is place it hees han' on de latch,
Dat's Isidore Goulay, las' fall on de Brulé
　　He's tak' it firs' prize on de grand ploughin'
　　　　match.

Ha! ha! Philomène!—dat was smart trick you play us
　　Come help de young feller tak' snow from
　　　　hees neck,
Dere's not'ing for hinder you come off de winder
　　W'en moon you was look for is come, I expec'—

Isidore, he is tole us de news on de parish
　　'Bout hees Lajeunesse Colt—travel two forty, sure,
'Bout Jeremie Choquette, come back from
　　　　Woonsocket
　　An' t'ree new leetle twin on Madame
　　　　Vaillancour'.

But nine o'clock strike, an' de chil'ren is sleepy,
     Mese'f an' ole woman can't stay up no more
So alone by de fire—'cos dey say dey ain't tire—
     We lef' Philomène an' de young Isidore.

I s'pose dey be talkin' beeg lot on de kitchen
     'Bout all de nice moon dey was see on de sky,
For Philomène's takin' long tam' get awaken
     Nex' day, she's so sleepy on bot' of de eye.

Dat's wan of dem t'ings, ev'ry tam' on de fashion,
     An' 'bout nices' t'ing dat was never be seen.
Got not'ing for say me—I spark it sam' way me
     W'en I go see de moder ma girl Philomène.

We leev very quiet 'way back on de contree
     Don't put on sam' style lak' de beeg village
W'en we don't get de monee you t'ink dat is fonny
     An' mak' plaintee sport on de Bottes Sauvages.

But I tole you—dat's true—I don't go on de city
     If you geev de fine house an' beaucoup d'argent—
I rader be stay me, an' spen' de las' day me
     On farm by de rapide dat's call Cheval Blanc.

Johnnie Courteau

Johnnie Courteau of de mountain
Johnnie Courteau of de hill
Dat was de boy can shoot de gun
Dat was de boy can jomp an' run
An' it's not very offen you ketch heem still
                    Johnnie Courteau!

Ax dem along de reever
Ax dem along de shore
Who was de mos' bes' fightin' man
From Managance to Shaw-in-i-gan?
De place w'ere de great beeg rapide roar,
                    Johnnie Courteau!

Sam' t'ing on ev'ry shaintee*
Up on de Mekinac
Who was de man can walk de log,
W'en w'ole of de reever she's black wit' fog
An' carry de beeges' load on hees back?
                    Johnnie Courteau!

* Shanty.

38

On de rapide you want to see heem
If de raf' she's swingin' roun'
An' he's yellin' "Hooraw Bateese! good man!"
W'y de oar come double on hees han'
W'en he's makin' dat raf' go flyin' down
                              Johnnie Courteau!

An' Tête de Boule chief can tole you
De feller w'at save hees life
W'en beeg moose ketch heem up a tree
Who's shootin' dat moose on de head, sapree!
An' den run off wit' hees Injun wife?
                              Johnnie Courteau!

An' he only have pike pole wit' heem
On Lac à la Tortue
W'en he meet de bear comin' down de hill
But de bear very soon is get hees fill!
An' he sole dat skin for ten dollar too,
                              Johnnie Courteau!

Oh he never was scare for not'ing
Lak' de ole coureurs de bois,
But w'en he's gettin' hees winter pay
De bes' t'ing sure is kip out de way
For he's goin' right off on de Hip Hooraw!
                              Johnnie Courteau!

Den pullin' hees sash aroun' heem
He dance on hees botte sauvage
An' shout "All aboar' if you want to fight!"
Wall! you never can see de finer sight
W'en he go lak' dat on de w'ole village!
                        Johnnie Courteau!

But Johnnie Courteau get marry
On Philomène Beaurepaire
She 's nice leetle girl was run de school
On w'at you call Parish of Sainte Ursule
An' he see her off on de pique-nique dere
                        Johnnie Courteau!

Den somet'ing come over Johnnie
W'en he marry on Philomène
For he stay on de farm de w'ole year roun'
He chop de wood an' he plough de groun'
An' he 's quieter feller was never seen,
                        Johnnie Courteau!

An' ev'ry wan feel astonish
From la Tuque to Shaw-in-i-gan
W'en dey hear de news was goin' aroun'
Along on de reever up an' down
How wan leetle woman boss dat beeg man
                        Johnnie Courteau!

He never come out on de evening
No matter de hard we try
'Cos he stay on de kitchen an' sing hees song
> *A la claire fontaine,*
> *M'en allant promener,*
> *J'ai trouvé l'eau si belle*
> *Que je m'y suis baigner!*
> *Lui y'a longtemps que je t'aime*
> *Jamais je ne t'oublierai.*

Rockin' de cradle de w'ole night long
Till baby 's asleep on de sweet bimeby
> Johnnie Courteau!

An' de house, wall! I wish you see it
De place she 's so nice an' clean
Mus' wipe your foot on de outside door,
You 're dead man sure if you spit on de floor,
An' he never say not'ing on Philomène,
> Johnnie Courteau!

An' Philomène watch de monee
An' put it all safe away
On very good place; I dunno w'ere
But anyhow noboddy see it dere
So she 's buyin' new farm de noder day
> *Madame* Courteau!

Phil-o-rum's Canoe

"O ma ole canoe! w'at 's matter wit' you,
      an' w'y was you be so slow?
Don't I work hard enough on de paddle, an'
      still you don't seem to go—
No win' at all on de fronte side, an' current
      she don't be strong,
Den w'y are you lak' lazy feller, too sleepy for
      move along?

"I 'member de tam' w'en you jomp de sam 'as
      deer wit' de wolf behin'
An' brochet on de top de water, you scare
      heem mos' off hees min';
But fish don't care for you now at all, only jus'
      mebbe wink de eye,
For he know it 's easy git out de way w'en you
      was a passin' by."

I'm spikin 'dis way jus' de oder day w'en I'm
      out wit' de ole canoe,
Crossin' de point w'ere I see las' fall wan very
      beeg caribou,
W'en somebody say, "Phil-o-rum, mon vieux,
      wat 's matter wit' you youse'f?"
An' who do you s'pose was talkin'? w'y de
      poor ole canoe shese'f.

O yass, I 'm scare w'en I 'm sittin' dere, an'
      she 's callin' ma nam' dat way:
"Phil-o-rum Juneau, w'y you spik so moche,
      you 're off on de head today.
Can't be you forget ole feller, you an' me
      we 're not too young,
An' if I 'm lookin' so ole lak' you, I t'ink I
      will close ma tongue.

"You should feel ashame; for you 're alway
      blame, w'en it is n't ma fault at all
For I 'm tryin' to do bes' I can for you on
      summer-tam', spring, an' fall.
How offen you drown on de reever if I 'm not
      lookin' out for you
W'en you 're takin' too moche on de w'isky
      some night comin' down de Soo.

"De firs' tam' we go on de Wessoneau no
      feller can beat us den,
For you 're purty strong man wit' de paddle,
      but dat 's long ago ma frien',
An' win' she can blow off de mountain, an'
      tonder an' rain may come,
But camp see us bot' on de evening—you
      know dat was true, Phil-o-rum.

"An' who 's your horse too, but your ole
      canoe, an' w'en you feel cole an' wet
Who was your house w'en I 'm upside down
      an' onder de roof you get,
Wit' rain ronnin' down ma back, Baptême!
      till I 'm gettin' de rheumateez,
An' I never say not'ing at all, moi-même, but
      let you do jus' you please.

"You t'ink it was right, kip me out all night
      on reever side down below,
An' even 'Bon Soir' you was never say, but
      off on de camp you go
Leffin' your poor ole canoe behin' lyin' dere
      on de groun'
Watchin' de moon on de water, an' de bat
      flyin' all aroun'.

"O! dat 's lonesome t'ing hear de grey owl
　　　sing up on de beeg pine tree
An' many long night she kip me awake till
　　　on de eas' I see,
An' den you come down on de morning for
　　　start on some more voyage.
An' only t'ing decen' you do all day is carry
　　　me on portage.

"Dat 's way, Phil-o-rum, rheumateez she
　　　come, wit' pain ronnin' troo ma side
Wan leetle hole here, noder beeg wan dere,
　　　dat not'ing can never hide;
Don't do any good fix me up again, no
　　　matter how moche you try,
For w'en we come ole an' our work she 's
　　　done, bot' man an' canoe mus' die."

Wall! she talk dat way mebbe mos' de day,
　　　till we 're passin' some beaver dam
An' wan de young beaver he 's mak' hees tail
　　　come down on de water flam!
I never see de canoe so scare, she jomp nearly
　　　two, t'ree feet
I t'ink she was goin' for ronne away, an' she
　　　shut up de mout' toute suite.

It mak' me feel queer, de strange t'ing I hear,
 an' I 'm glad she don't spik no more,
But soon as we fin' ourse'f arrive over dere on
 de noder shore
I tak' dat canoe lak' de lady, an' carry her off
 wit' me,
For I 'm sorry de way I treat her, an' she know
 more dan me, sapree!

Yass! dat 's smart canoe, an' I know it 's true,
 w'at she 's spikin' wit' me dat day,
I 'm not de young feller I use to be w'en work
 she was only play;
An' I know I was comin' closer on place w'ere
 I mus' tak' care
W'ere de mos' worse current 's de las' wan too,
 de current of Dead Rivière.

You can only steer, an' if rock be near, wit
 wave dashin' all aroun',
Better mak' leetle prayer, for on Dead Rivière
 some very smart man get drown;
But if you be locky an' watch youse'f, mebbe
 reever won't seem so wide,
An' firs' t'ing you know you 'll ronne ashore,
 safe on de noder side.

Le Vieux Temps

Venez ici, mon cher ami, an' sit down by
      me—so
An' I will tole you story of old tam' long ago—
W'en ev'ryt'ing is happy—w'en all de bird is sing
An' me!—I'm young an' strong lak' moose
      an' not afraid no t'ing.

I close my eye jus' so, an' see de place w'ere
      I am born—
I close my ear an' lissen to musique of de horn,
Dat's horn ma dear ole moder blow—an
      only t'ing she play
Is "viens donc vite Napoléon—'pêche toi
      pour votre souper."

An' wen he 's hear dat nice musique – ma
      leetle dog "Carleau"
Is place hees tail upon hees back – an' den he 's
      let heem go –
He 's jomp on fence – he 's swimmin' crik –
      he 's ronne two forty gait,
He say "dat 's somet'ing good for eat – Carleau
      mus' not be late."

O dem was pleasure day for sure, dem day o
      long ago
W'en I was play wit' all de boy, an' all de girl
      also;
An' many tam' w'en I 'm alone an' t'ink of day
      gone by
An' pull latire* an' spark de girl, I cry upon
      my eye.

Ma fader an' moder too, got nice, nice
      familee,
Dat 's ten garçon an' t'orteen girl, was mak'
      it twenty t'ree
But fonny t'ing de Gouvernement don't geev
      de firs' prize den
Lak w'at dey say dey geev it now, for only
      wan douzaine.
* *Taffy pull.*

De English peop' dat only got wan familee
        small size
Mus' be feel glad dat tam' dere is no honder'
        acre prize
For fader of twelve chil'ren—dey know dat
        mus' be so,
De Canayens would boss Kebeck—mebbe
        Ontario.

But dat is not de story dat I was gone tole
        you
About de fun we use to have w'en we leev
        à chez nous
We're never lonesome on dat house, for
        many cavalier
Come at our place mos' every night—
        especially Sun-day.

But tam' I 'member bes' is w'en I 'm twenty-
        wan year—me—
An' so for mak' some pleasurement—we geev
        wan large soirée
De whole paroisse she be invite—de Curé
        he 's come too—
Wit plaintee peop' from 'noder place—
        dat 's more I can tole you.

De night she's cole an' freeze also, chemin
      she's fill wit snow
An' on de chimley lak' phantome, de win' is
      mak' it blow—
But boy an' girl come all de sam' an' pass on
      grande parloir
For warm itself on beeg box stove, was mak'
      on Trois Rivières—

An' w'en Bonhomme Latour commence for
      tune up hees fidelle
It mak' us all feel very glad—l' enfant! he
      play so well,
Musique suppose to be firs' class, I offen hear,
      for sure
But mos' bes' man, beat all de res', is ole
      Bateese Latour—

An' w'en Bateese play Irish jeeg, he's learn on
      Mattawa
Dat tam' he's head boss cook Shaintee—den
      leetle Joe Leblanc
Tak' hole de beeg Marie Juneau an' dance
      upon de floor
Till Marie say "Excuse to me, I cannot dance
      no more."

An' den de Curé 's mak' de speech—ole Curé
      Ladouceur!
He say de girl was spark de boy too much on
      some cornerre—
An' so he 's tole Bateese play up ole fashion
      reel à quatre
An' every boddy she mus' dance, dey can't
      get off on dat.

Away she go—hooraw! hooraw! plus fort
      Bateese, mon vieux
Camille Bisson, please watch your girl—dat 's
      bes' t'ing you can do,
Pass on de right an' tak' your place Mamzelle
      Des Trois Maisons
You 're s'pose for dance on Paul Laberge, not
      Telesphore Gagnon.

Mon oncle Alfred, he spik lak' dat—'cos he
      is boss de floor,
An' so we do our possibill an' den commence
      encore.
Dem crowd of boy an' girl I 'm sure kip up
      until nex' day
If ole Bateese don't stop hese'f, he come so
      fatigué.

An' affer dat, we eat some t'ing, tak' leetle
    drink also
An' de Curè, he's tole story of many year
    ago—
W'en Iroquois sauvage she's keel de Canayens
    an' steal deir hair,
An' say dat's only for Bon Dieu, we don't
    be here—he don't be dere.

But dat was mak' de girl feel scare—so all de
    cavalier
Was ax hees girl go home right off, an' place
    her on de sleigh,
An' w'en dey start, de Curé say, "Bonsoir et
    bon voyage
Ménagez-vous—tak' care for you—prenez
    garde pour les sauvages."

An' den I go mese'f also, an' tak' ma belle
    Elmire—
She's nicer girl on whole Comté, an' jus' got
    eighteen year—
Black hair—black eye, an' chick rosèe dat's
    lak' wan fameuse on de fall
But do n't spik much—not of dat kin', I can't
    say she love me at all.

Ma girl—she's fader beeg farmeur—leev
       'noder side St. Flore
Got five-six honder' acre—mebbe a leetle
       more—
Nice sugar bush—une belle maison—de bes' I
       never see—
So w'en I go for spark Elmire, I don't be
       mak' de foolish me—

Elmire!—she's pass t'ree year on school—
       Ste. Anne de la Perade
An' w'en she's tak' de firs' class prize, dat's
       mak' de ole man glad;
He say "Ba gosh—ma girl can wash—can
       keep de kitchen clean
Den change her dress—mak' politesse before
       God save de Queen."

Dey's many way for spark de girl, an' you
       know dat of course,
Some way dey might be better way, an'
       some dey might be worse
But I lak' sit some cole night wit' my girl on
       ole burleau
Wit' lot of hay keep our foot warm—an'
       plaintee buffalo—

Dat 's geev good chances get acquaint—an' if
  burleau upset
An' t'row you out upon de snow—dat 's
  better chances yet—
An' if you help de girl go home, if horse he
  ronne away
De girl she 's not much use at all—don't geev
  you nice baiser!

Dat 's very well for fun ma frien', but w'en
  you spark for keep
She 's not sam' t'ing an' mak' you feel so
  scare lak' leetle sheep
Some tam' you get de fever—some tam'
  you 're lak' snowball
An' all de tam' you ack lak' fou—can't spik
  no t'ing at all.

Wall! dat 's de way I feel mese'f, wit
  Elmire on burleau,
Jus' lak' small dog try ketch hees tail—
  roun' roun' ma head she go
But bimeby I come more brave—an' tak'
  Elmire she's han'
"Laisse-moi tranquille" Elmire she say
  "You mus' be crazy man."

"Yass—yass" I say "Mebbe you t'ink I'm
  wan beeg loup garou,
Dat's forty t'ousand 'noder girl, I lef' dem all
  for you,
Is'pose you know Polique Gauthier your
  frien' on St. Cesaire
Jax her marry me nex' wick—she tak' me—I
  don't care."

Ba gosh; Elmire she don't lak' dat—it mak'
  her feel so mad—
She commence cry, say " 'Poléon you treat
  me very bad—
I don't lak' see you t'row you'se'f upon Polique
  Gauthier,
So if you say you love me sure—we mak'
  de marieé."

Oh it was fine tam' affer dat—Castor I t'ink he
  know,
We 're not too busy for get home—he go so
  nice an' slow,
He 's only upset t'ree—four tam'—an' jus'
  about daylight
We pass upon de ole man's place—an' every
  t'ing 's all right.

Wall! we leev happy on de farm for nearly
      fifty year,
Till wan day on de summer tam'—she die—
      ma belle Elmire.
I feel so lonesome lef'behind'—I t'ink 't was
      bes' mebbe—
Dat w'en le Bon Dieu tak' ma famme—he
      should not forget me.

But dat is hees biz/nesse ma frien'—I know
      dat's all right dere
I'll wait till he call " 'Poléon" den I will be
      prepare—
An' w'en he fin' me ready, for mak' de longue
      voyage
He guide me t'roo de wood hese'f upon ma
      las' portage.

The Canadian Country Doctor

I s'pose mos' ev'ry boddy t'ink hees job 's
    about de hardes'
  From de boss man on de Gouvernement
    to poor man on de town
From de curé to de lawyer, an' de farmer to
    de school boy
An' all de noder feller was mak' de worl' go
    roun'.

But dere 's wan man got hees han' full t'roo
    ev'ry kin' of wedder
  An' he 's never sure of not'ing but work
    an' work away—
Dat 's de man dey call de doctor, w'en you
    ketch heem on de contree
  An' he 's only man I know me, don't got
    no holiday.

If you 're comin off de city spen de summer
     tam' among us
    An' you walk out on de mornin w'en de
     leetle bird is sing
Mebbe den you see de doctor w'en he 's
     passin' wit' hees buggy
    An' you t'ink "Wall! contree doctor mus'
     be very pleasan' t'ing.

"Drivin' dat way all de summer up an' down
     along de reever
    W'ere de nice cool win' is blowin' among
     de maple tree
Den w'en he 's mak' hees visit, comin'
     home before de night tam'
For pass de quiet evening wit' hees wife an'
     familee."

An' w'en off across de mountain, some wan 's
     sick an' want de doctor
    "Mus' be fine trip crossin' over for watch
     de sun go down
Makin' all dem purty colour lak' w'at you call
     de rainbow,"
    Dat 's way de peop' is talkin' was leevin'
     on de town.

But it is n't alway summer on de contree, an
      de doctor
   He could tole you many story of de storm
      dat he 's been in
How hees coonskin coat come handy, w'en
      de win' blow off de reever
   For if she 's sam' ole reever, she 's not
      alway sam' old win'.

An' de mountain dat 's so quiet w'en de w'ite
      cloud go a sailin'
   All about her on de summer w'ere de
      sheep is feedin' high
You should see her on December w'en de
      snow is pilin' roun' her
   An' all de win' of winter come tearin'
      t'roo de sky.

O! le bon Dieu help de doctor w'en de
      message come to call heem
   From hees warm bed on de night tam'
      for visit some poor man
Lyin' sick across de hill side on noder side de
      reever
   An' he hear de mountain roarin' lak' de
      beeg Shawinigan.

Ah! well he know de warning but he can't
    stay till de morning
    So he 's hitchin' up hees leetle horse an'
      put heem on burleau
Den w'en he 's feex de buffalo, an' wissle to
    hees pony
    Away t'roo storm an' hurricane de contree
      doctor go.

O! de small Canadian pony! dat 's de horse
    can walk de snowdreef'
    Dat 's de horse can fin' de road too he 's
      never been before
Kip your heart up leetle feller, for dere 's
    many mile before you
    An' it 's purty hard job tellin' w'en you
      see your stable door.

Yass! de doctor he can tole you, if he have de
    tam for talkin'
    All about de bird was singin' before de
      summer lef'
For he 's got dem on hees bureau an' he 's
    doin' it hese'f too
    An' de las' tam' I was dere, me, I see dem
      all mese'f.

But about de way he travel t'roo de stormy
      night of winter
    W'en de rain come on de spring flood, an'
      de bridge is wash away
All de hard work, all de danger dat was offen
      hang aroun' heem
    Dat's de tam' our contree doctor don't
      have very moche to say.

For it's purty ole, ole story, an' he alway have
      it wit' heem
    Ever since he come among us on parish
      Saint Mathieu
An' no doubt he's feelin' mebbe jus' de sam'
      as noder feller
    So he rader do hees talkin' about somet'ing
      dat was new.

The Curé of Calumette

*The Curé of a French-Canadian parish, when
summoned to the bedside of a dying member of his
flock, always carries in his buggy or sleigh a bell.
This bell serves two purposes: first, it has the effect
of clearing a way for the passage of the good priest's
vehicle, and, secondly, it calls to prayer those of the
faithful who are within bearing of its solemn tones.*

Dere 's no voyageur on de reever never run
      hees canoe d'écorce*
T'roo de roar an' de rush of de rapide, w'ere it
      jump lak' a beeg w'ite horse,
Dere 's no hunter man on de prairie, never
      wear w'at you call racquette
Can beat leetle Fader O'Hara, de Curé of
      Calumette.
* *Birchbark canoe.*

Hees fader is full-blooded Irish, an' hees
      moder is pure Canayenne,
Not offen dat stock go togedder, but she's
      fine combination ma frien'
For de Irish he's full of de devil, an' de
      French dey got savoir faire,
Dat's mak' it de very good balance an' tak'
      you mos' ev'ry w'ere.

But dere's wan t'ing de Curé wont stan' it;
      mak' fun on de Irlandais
An' of course on de French we say not'ing, 'cos
      de parish she's all Canayen,
Den you see on account of de moder, he can't
      spik hese'f very moche,
So de ole joke she's all out of fashion, an'
      wan of dem t'ing we don't touch.

Wall! wan of dat kin' is de Curé, but w'en he
      be comin' our place
De peop' on de parish all w'isper, "How
      young he was look on hees face;
Too bad if de wedder she keel heem de firs
      tam' he got leetle wet,
An' de Bishop might sen' beeger Curé, for
      it's purty tough place, Calumette!"

Ha! ha! how I wish I was dere, me, w'en he
      go on de mission call
On de shaintee camp way up de reever, drivin
      hees own cariole,
An' he meet blaggar' feller been drinkin', jus'
      enough mak' heem ack lak' fou,
Joe Vadeboncoeur, dey was call heem, an
      he's purty beeg feller too!

Mebbe Joe he don't know it's de Curé, so
      he's hollerin', "Get out de way,
If you don't geev me whole of de roadside,
      sapree! you go off on de sleigh."
But de Curé he never say not'ing, jus' poule on
      de line leetle bit,
An' w'en Joe try for kip heem hees promise,
      hees nose it get badly hit.

Maudit! he was strong leetle Curé, an' he go
      for Jo-zeph en masse
An' w'en he is mak' it de finish, poor Joe is n't
      feel it firs' class,
So nex' tam' de Curé he's goin' for visit de
      shaintee encore
Of course he was mak' beeges' mission never
      see on dat place before.

An' he know more, I'm sure dan de lawyer,
     an' dere's many poor habitant
Is glad for see Fader O'Hara, an' ax w'at he
     t'ink of de law
W'en dey get leetle troub' wit' each oder, an'
     don't know de bes' t'ing to do,
Dat's makin' dem save plaintee monee, an'
     kip de good neighbour too.

But w'en we fin' out how he paddle till canoe
     she was nearly fly
An' travel racquette on de winter, w'en
     snowdreef' is pilin' up high
For visit some poor man or woman dat's
     waitin' de message of peace,
An' get dem prepare for de journey, we're
     proud on de leetle pries'!

O! many dark night w'en de chil'ren is put
     away safe on de bed
An' mese'f an' ma femme mebbe sittin' an'
     watchin, de small curly head
We hear somet'ing else dan de roar of de
     tonder, de win' an' de rain;
So we're bot' passin' out on de doorway, an'
     lissen an' lissen again.

An' it 's lonesome for see de beeg cloud
        sweepin' across de sky
An' lonesome for hear de win' cryin' lak'
        somebody 's goin' to die,
But de soun' away down de valley, creepin'
        aroun' de hill
All de tam' gettin' closer, closer, dat 's de
        soun' mak' de heart stan' still!

It 's de bell of de leetle Curé, de music of
        deat' we hear,
Along on de black road ringin', an' soon it
        was comin' near
Wan minute de face of de Curé we see by de
        lantern light,
An' he 's gone from us, jus' lak' a shadder,
        into de stormy night.

An' de buggy rush down de hill side an' over
        de bridge below,
W'ere creek run so high on de spring tam',
        w'en mountain t'row off de snow,
An' so long as we hear heem goin', we kneel
        on de floor an' pray
Dat God will look affer de Curé, an' de poor
        soul dat 's passin' away.

I dunno if he need our prayer, but we geev it
      heem jus' de sam',
For w'en a man 's doin' hees duty lak' de
      Curé do all de tam'
Never min' all de t'ing may happen, no
      matter he 's riche or poor
Le bon Dieu was up on de heaven, will look
      out for dat man, I 'm sure.

I 'm only poor habitant farmer, an' mebbe
      know not'ing at all,
But dere 's wan t'ing I 'm alway wishin', an'
      dat 's w'en I get de call
For travel de far-away journey, ev'ry wan on
      de worl' mus' go
He 'll be wit' me de leetle Curé 'fore I 'm
      leffin' dis place below.

For I know I 'll be feel more easy, if he 's
      sittin' dere by de bed
An' he 'll geev me de good-bye message, an'
      place hees han' on ma head,
Den I 'll hol' if he 'll only let me, dat han' till
      de las' las' breat'
An' bless leetle Fader O'Hara, de Curé of
      Calumette.

De Stove Pipe Hole

Dat's very cole an' stormy night on Village
      St. Mathieu,
W'en ev'ry wan he's go couché, an' dog was
      quiet, too—
Young Dominique is start heem out see
      Emmeline Gourdon,
Was leevin' on her fader's place, Maxime de
      Forgeron.

Poor Dominique he's lak' dat girl, an' love
      her mos' de tam',
An' she was mak' de promise—sure—some
      day she be his famme,
But she have worse old fader dat's never on de
      worl',
Was swear onless he's riche lak' diable, no
      feller's get hees girl.

He's mak' it plaintee fuss about hees
      daughter Emmeline,
Dat's mebbe nice girl, too, but den, Mon
      Dieu, she's not de Queen!
An' w'en de young man's come aroun' for
      spark it on de door,
An' hear de ole man swear "Baptême!" he's
      never come no more.

Young Dominique he's sam' de res'—was scare
      for ole Maxime,
He don't lak' risk hese'f too moche for chances
      seein' heem,
Dat's only stormy night he come, so dark
      you cannot see,
An dat's de reason w'y also, he's climb de
      gallerie.

De girl she's waitin' dere for heem—don't
      care about de rain,
So glad for see young Dominique he's comin'
      back again,
Dey bot' forget de ole Maxime, an' mak' de
      embrasser
An affer dey was finish dat, poor Dominique
      is say—

"Good-bye, dear Emmeline, good-bye; I'm
      goin' very soon,
For you I got no better chance, dan feller on
      de moon—
It's all de fault your fader, too, dat I be go
      away,
He's got no use for me at all—I see dat ev'ry
      day.

"He's never meet me on de road but he is
      say 'Sapree!'
An' if he ketch me on de house I'm scare he's
      killin' me,
So I mus' lef' ole St. Mathieu, for work on
      'noder place,
An' till I mak de beeg for-tune, you never
      see ma face."

Den Emmeline say "Dominique, ma love
      you'll alway be
An' if you kiss me two, t'ree tam' I'll not
      tole noboddy—
But prenez garde ma fader, please, I know
      he's gettin' ole—
All sam' he offen walk de house upon de
      stockin' sole.

"Good-bye, good-bye, cher Dominique! I
      know you will be true,
I don't want no riche feller me, ma heart she
      go wit' you,"
Dat's very quick he's kiss her den, before de
      fader come,
But don't get too moche pleasurement—so
      'fraid de ole Bonhomme.

Wall! jus' about dey're half way t'roo wit all
      dat love beez-nesse
Emmeline say, "Dominique, w'at for you're
      scare lak' all de res'?
Don't see mese'f moche danger now de ole man
      come aroun','"
W'en minute affer dat, dere's noise, lak'
      house she's fallin' down.

Den Emmeline she holler "Fire! will no wan
      come for me?"
An Dominique is jomp so high, near bus'
      de gallerie—
"Help! help! right off," somebody shout,
      "I'm killin' on ma place,
It's all de fault ma daughter, too, dat girl
      she's ma disgrace."

He's kip it up long tam' lak' dat, but not
        hard tellin' now,
W'at 's all de noise upon de house—who 's
        kick heem up de row?
It seem Bonhomme was sneak aroun' upon de
        stockin' sole,
An' firs' t'ing den de ole man walk right
        t'roo de stove pipe hole.

W'en Dominique is see heem dere, wit' wan
        leg hang below,
An' 'noder leg straight out above, he 's glad
        for ketch heem so—
De ole man can't do not'ing, den, but swear
        and ax for w'y
Noboddy tak' heem out dat hole before he 's
        comin' die.

Den Dominique he spik lak' dis, "Mon cher
        M'sieur Gourdon
I 'm not riche city feller, me, I 'm only
        habitant,
But I was love more I can tole your daughter
        Emmeline,
An' if I marry on dat girl, Bagosh! she 's lak'
        de Queen.

"I want you mak' de promise now, before it's
      come too late,
An' I mus' tole you dis also, dere's not
      moche tam' for wait.
Your foot she's hangin' down so low, I'm
      'fraid she ketch de cole,
Wall! if you give me Emmeline, I pull you
      out de hole."

Dat mak' de ole man swear more hard he
      never swear before,
An' wit' de foot he's got above, he's kick it
      on de floor,
"Non, non," he say "Sapré tonnerre! she
      never marry you,
An' if you don't look out you get de jail on
      St. Mathieu."

"Correc'," young Dominique is say, "mebbe
      de jail's tight place,
But you got wan small corner, too, I see it on
      de face,
So if you don't lak' geev de girl on wan poor
      habitant,
Dat's be mese'f, I say, Bonsoir, mon cher
      M'sieur Gourdon."

"Come back, come back," Maxime is
   shout—"I promise you de girl,
I never see no wan lak' you—no never on de
   worl'!
It 's not de nice trick you was play on man
   dat 's gettin' ole,
But do jus' w'at you lak', so long you pull me
   out de hole."

"Hooraw! Hooraw!" Den Dominique is pull
   heem out toute suite
An' Emmeline she 's helpin' too for place
   heem on de feet,
An' affer dat de ole man 's tak' de young
   peop' down de stair,
W'ere he is go couchè right off, an' dey go on
   parloir.

Nex' Sunday morning dey was call by
   M'sieur le Curé.
Get marry soon, an' ole Maxime geev
   Emmeline away;
Den affer dat dey settle down lak' habitant is
   do,
An' have de mos' fine familee on Village St.
   Mathieu.

Dreams

Bord à Plouffe, Bord à Plouffe,
W'at do I see w'en I dream of you?
A shore w'ere de water is racin' by,
A small boy lookin', an' wonderin' w'y
He can't get fedder for goin' fly
Lak' de hawk makin' ring on de summer sky,
      Dat 's w'at I see.

Bord à Plouffe, Bord à Plouffe,
W'at do I hear w'en I dream of you?
Too many t'ing for sleepin' well!
De song of de ole tam' cariole bell,
De voice of dat girl from Sainte Angèle
(I geev her a ring was mark "fidèle")
      Dat 's w'at I hear.

Bord à Plouffe, Bord à Plouffe,
W'at do I smoke w'en I dream of you?
Havana cigar from across de sea,
An' get dem for not'ing too? No siree!
Dere's only wan kin' of tabac for me.
An' it grow on de Rivière des Prairies—
    Dat's w'at I smoke.

Bord à Plouffe, Bord à Plouffe,
How do I feel w'en I t'ink of you?
Sick, sick for de ole place way back dere—
An' to sleep on ma own leetle room upstair
W'ere de ghos' on de chimley mak' me scare
I'd geev more monee dan I can spare—
    Dat's how I feel.

Bord à Plouffe, Bord à Plouffe,
W'at will I do w'en I'm back wit' you?
I'll buy de farm of Bonhomme Martel,
Long tam' he's been waitin' a chance to sell,
Den pass de nex' morning on Sainte Angèle,
An, if she's not marry—dat girl—very well,
    Dat's w'at I'll do.

De Snowbird

O leetle bird dat's come to us w'en
    stormy win' she's blowin',
  An' ev'ry fiel' an' mountain top is cover
    wit' de snow,
How far from home you're flyin', noboddy's
    never knowin'
  For spen' wit' us de winter tam', mon
    cher petit oiseau!

We alway know you're comin', w'en we
    hear de firs' beeg storm,
  A sweepin' from de sky above, an'
    screamin' as she go—
Can tell you're safe inside it, w'ere you're
    keepin' nice an' warm,
  But no wan's never see you dere, mon
    cher petit oiseau!

Was it 'way behin' de mountain, dat de nort'
  win' ketch you sleepin'
    Mebbe on your leetle nes' too, an' before
    de wing she grow,
Lif' you up an' bring you dat way, till some
  morning fin' you peepin'
    Out of new nes' on de snow dreef', mon
    pauv' petit oiseau!

All de wood is full on summer, wit' de many
  bird is sing dere,
    Dey mus' offen know each oder, mebbe
    mak' de frien' also,
But w'en you was come on winter, never
  seein' wan strange wing dere
    Was it mak' you feelin' lonesome, mon
    pauv' petit oiseau?

Plaintee bird is alway hidin' on some place
  no wan can fin' dem,
    But me leetle bird of winter, dat was not
    de way you go—
For de chil'ren on de roadside, you don't seem
  to care for min' dem
    W'en dey pass on way to schoolhouse,
    mon cher petit oiseau!

No wan say you sing lak' robin, but you got
      no tam' for singin'
  So busy it was keepin' you get breakfas' on
      de snow,
But de small note you was geev us, w'en it
      join de sleigh bell ringin'
  Mak' de true Canadian music, mon cher
      petit oiseau!

O de long an' lonesome winter, if you 're
      never comin' near us'
  If we miss you on de roadside, an' on all de
      place below!
But le bon Dieu he will sen' you t'roo de
      storm again for cheer us,
  W'en we mos' was need you here too,
      mon cher petit oiseau!

Memories

O spirit of the mountain that speaks to us
      tonight,
Your voice is sad, yet still recalls past visions
      of delight,
When 'mid the grand old Laurentides, old
      when the earth was new,
With flying feet we followed the moose and
      caribou.

And backward rush sweet memories, like
      fragments of a dream,
We hear the dip of paddle blades, the ripple of
      the stream,
The mad, mad rush of frightened wings from
      brake and covert start,
The breathing of the woodland, the throb of
      nature's heart.

Once more beneath our eager feet the forest
    carpet springs,
We march through gloomy valleys, where
    the vesper sparrow sings.
The little minstrel heeds us not, nor stays his
    plaintive song,
As with our brave coureurs de bois we swiftly
    pass along.

Again o'er dark Wayagamack, in bark canoe
    we glide,
And watch the shades of evening glance along
    the mountain side.
Anon we hear resounding the wizard loon's
    wild cry,
And mark the distant peak whereon the
    ling'ring echoes die.

But Spirit of the Northland! let the winter
    breezes blow,
And cover every giant crag with rifts of
    driving snow.
Freeze every leaping torrent, bind all the
    crystal lakes,
Tell us of fiercer pleasures when the Storm
    King awakes.

And now the vision changes, the winds are
      loud and shrill,
The falling flakes are shrouding the
      mountain and the hill,
But safe within our snug cabane with
      comrades gathered near,
We set the rafters ringing with "Roulant"
      and "Brigadier."

Then after Pierre and Telesphore have danced
      "Le Caribou,"
Some hardy trapper tells a tale of the dreaded
      Loup Garou,
Or phantom bark in moonlit heavens, with
      prow turned to the East,
Bringing the Western voyageurs to join the
      Christmas feast.

And while each backwoods troubadour is
      greeted with huzza
Slowly the homely incense of "tabac
      Canayen"
Rises and sheds its perfume like flowers of
      Araby,
O'er all the true-born loyal Enfants de la
      Patrie.

And thus with song and story, with laugh
     and jest and shout,
We heed not dropping mercury nor storms
     that rage without,
But pile the huge logs higher till the chimney
     roars with glee,
And banish spectral visions with La
     Chanson Normandie.

    Brigadier! répondit Pandore
    Brigadier! vous avez raison,
    Brigadier! répondit Pandore,
    Brigadier! vous avez raison!

O spirit of the mountain! that speaks to us
     tonight,
Return again and bring us new dreams of past
     delight,
And while our heart-throbs linger, and till
     our pulses cease,
We 'll worship thee among the hills where
     flows the Saint-Maurice.

Getting Stout

Eighteen, an' face lak' de—w'at 's de good?
    Dere 's no use tryin' explain
De way she 's lookin', dat girl Marie—
    But affer it pass, de rain,
An' sun come out of de cloud behin',
    An' laugh on de sky wance more—
Wall! dat is de way her eye it shine
    W'en she see me upon de door.

An' dere she 's workin' de ole tam' sash,
    De fines' wan, too, for sure.
"Who is it for, ma belle Marie—
    You 're makin' de nice ceinture?
Come out an' sit on de shore below,
    For watchin' dem draw de net,
Ketchin' de feesh," an' she answer, "No,
    De job is n't finish yet;

"Stan' up, Narcisse, an' we'll see de fit.
    Dat sash it was mak' for you,
For de ole wan's gettin' on, you know,
    An' o' course it'll never do
If de boy I marry can't go an spen'
    W'at dey're callin' de weddin' tour
Wit' me, for visitin' all hees frien',
    An' not have a nice ceinture."

An' den she measure dat sash on me,
    An' I fin' it so long an' wide
I pass it aroun' her, an' dere we stan',
    De two of us bot' inside—
"Could n't be better, ma chère Marie,
    Dat sash it is fit so well—
It jus' suit you, an' it jus' suit me,
    An' bot' togeder, ma belle."

So I wear it off on de weddin' tour
    An' long affer dat also,
An' never a minute I'm carin' how
    De win' of de winter blow—
Don't matter de cole an' frosty night—
    Don't matter de stormy day,
So long as I'm feex up close an' tight
    Wit' de ole ceinture fleché.

An' w'ere 's de woman can beat her now,
    Ma own leetle girl Marie?
For we 're marry today jus' feefty year
    An' never a change I see—
But wan t'ing strange, dough I try ma bes'
    For measure dat girl wance more,
She say—"Go off wit' de foolishness,
    Or pass on de outside door.

"You know well enough dat sash get tight
    Out on de snow an' wet
Drivin' along on ev'ry place,
    Den how can it fit me yet?
Shows w'at a fool you be, Narcisse,
    W'enever you go to town;
Better look out, or I call de pries'
    For makin' you stan' aroun'."

But me, I 'm sure it was never change,
    Dat sash on de feefty year—
An' I can't understan' today at all,
    W'at 's makin' it seem so queer—
De sash is de sam', an' woman too,
    Can't fool me, I know too well—
But woman, of course dey offen do
    Some funny t'ing—you can't tell!

We 're Irish Yet

What means this gathering tonight?
　　What spirit moves along
The crowded hall, and, touching light
　　Each heart among the throng,
Awakes, as tho' a trumpet blast
　　Had sounded in their ears,
The recollections of the past,
　　The memories of the years?

Oh! 't is the spirit of the West,
　　The spirit of the Celt,
The breed that spurned the alien breast
　　And every wrong has felt—
And still, tho' far from fatherland,
　　We never can forget
To tell ourselves, with heart and hand,
　　We 're Irish yet! We 're Irish yet!

And they outside the clan of Conn
    Would understand, but fail,
The mystic music played upon
    The heart-strings of the Gael—
His ear, and his alone, can tell
    The soul that lies within,
The music which he knows so well,
    The voice of Kith and Kin.

He hears the tales of old, old days
    Of battle fierce by ford and hill,
Of ancient Senachie's martial lays,
    And race unconquered still.
It challenges with mother's pride
    And dares him to forget
That, tho' he cross the ocean wide,
    He 's Irish yet! He 's Irish yet!

His eye may never see the blue
    Of Ireland's April sky,
His ear may never listen to
    The song of lark on high,
But deep within his Irish heart
    Are cloisters, dark and dim,
No human hand can wrench apart,
    And the lark still sings for him.

We 've bowed beneath the chastening rod,
    We 've had our griefs and pains,
But with them all, we still thank God,
    The Blood is in our veins,
The ancient blood that knows no fear,
    The Stamp is on us set,
And so, however foes may jeer,
    We 're Irish yet! We 're Irish yet.

Meb-be

A quiet boy was Joe Bedotte,
    An' no sign anyw'ere
Of anyt'ing at all he got
    Is up to ordinaire—
An' w'en de teacher tell heem go
    An' tak' a holiday,
For wake heem up, becos' he's slow,
    Poor Joe would only say,
                "Wall! meb-be."

Don't bodder no wan on de school
    Unless dey bodder heem,
But all de scholar t'ink he's fool
    Or walkin' on a dream—
So w'en dey 're closin' on de spring
    Of course dey 're moche surprise
Dat Joe is takin' ev'ryt'ing
    Of w'at you call de prize.

An' den de teacher say, "Joseph,
   I know you 're workin' hard—
Becos' w'en I am pass mese'f
   I see you on de yard
A splittin' wood—no doubt you stay
   An' study half de night?"
An' Joe he spik de sam' ole way
  So quiet an' polite,

                 "Wall! meb be."

Hees fader an' hees moder die
   An' lef 'heem dere alone
Wit' chil'ren small enough to cry,
   An' farm all rock an' stone—
But Joe is fader, moder too,
   An' work bot' day an' night
An' clear de place—dat 's w'at he do,
   An' bring dem up all right.

De Curé say, "Joseph, you know
   Le bon Dieu 's very good—
He feed de small bird on de snow,
   De caribou on de wood—
But you deserve some credit too—
   I spik of dis before."
So Joe he dunno w'at to do
   An' only say wance more,

                 "Wall! meb be."

An' Joe he leev for many year
    An' helpin' ev'ry wan
Upon de parish far an' near
    Till all hees money 's gone—
An' den de Curé come again
    Wit' tear-drop on hees eye—
He know for sure poor Joe, hees frien',
    Is well prepare to die.

"Wall! Joe, de work you done will tell
    W'en you get up above—
De good God he will treat you well
    An' geev you all hees love.
De poor an' sick down here below,
    I 'm sure dey 'll not forget,"
An' w'at you t'ink he say, poor Joe,
    Drawin' hees only breat'?

                "Wall! meb-be."

Dominique

You dunno ma leetle boy Dominique?
 Never see heem runnin' roun' about de
  place?
'Cos I want to get advice how to kip heem
   lookin' nice,
  So he won't be alway dirty on de face—
Now dat leetle boy of mine, Dominique,
 If you wash heem an' you sen' heem off to
  school,
But instead of goin' dere, he was playin' fox
  an' hare—
  Can you tell me how to stop de leetle fool?

"I 'd tak' dat leetle feller Dominique,
 An' I 'd put heem on de cellar ev'ry day,
An' for workin' out a cure, bread an' water 's
  very sure,
  You can bet he mak' de promise not to
   play!"

Dat 's very well to say, but ma leetle Dominique
 W'en de jacket we put on heem 's only
  new,
An' he 's goin' travel roun' on de medder up
 an' down,
 Wit, de strawberry on hees pocket runnin'
  t'roo,
An' w'en he climb de fence, see de hole upon
  hees pant,
 No wonder hees poor moder 's feelin' mad!
So if you ketch heem den, w'at you want to
  do, ma frien' ?
 Tell me quickly an' before he get too bad.

"I 'd lick your leetle boy Dominique,
 I 'd lick heem till he 's cryin' purty hard,
An' for fear he 's gettin' spile, I 'd geev heem
  castor ile,
 An' I would n't let heem play outside de
  yard."

94

If you see ma leetle boy Dominique
    Hangin' on to poor ole "Billy" by de tail,
W'en dat horse is feelin' gay, lak' I see heem
      yesterday,
    I s'pose you t'ink he 's safer on de jail?
W'en I 'm lightin' up de pipe on de evenin'
      affer work,
    An' de powder dat young rascal 's puttin'
      in,
It was makin' such a pouf, nearly blow me
      t'roo de roof—
    W'at 's de way you got of showin' 't was a
      sin?

"Wall! I put heem on de jail right away,
    You may bet de wan is got de beeges' wall!
A honder' foot or so, w'ere dey never let heem
      go,
    Non! I would n't kip a boy lak' dat at
      all."

Dat 's good advice for sure, very good,
   On de cellar, bread an' water – it 'll do,
De nice sweet castor ile geev heem ev'ry
         leetle w'ile,
      An' de jail to finish up wit' w'en he 's
         t'roo!
Ah! ma frien', you never see Dominique,
   W'en he 's lyin' dere asleep upon de bed,
If you do, you say to me, "W'at an angel he
         mus' be,
      An' dere can't be not'ing bad upon hees
         head."

Many t'ank for your advice, an' it may be
         good for some,
      But de reason you was geev it is n't very
         hard to seek –
Yass! it 's easy seein' now w'en de talk is over,
         how
      You dunno ma leetle boy Dominique.

Bateese the Lucky Man

He's alway ketchin' doré, an' he's alway
    ketchin' trout
    On de place w'ere no wan else can ketch
      at all
He's alway ketchin' barbotte, dat's w'at you
    call bull-pout,
    An' he never miss de wil' duck on de fall.

O! de pa'tridge do some skippin' w'en she
    see heem on de swamp
    For she know Bateese don't go for
      not'ing dere,
An' de rabbit if he's comin', wall! you
    ought to see heem jomp.
    W'y he want to climb de tree he feel so
      scare.

Affer two hour by de reever I hear hees leetle
      song
   Den I meet heem all hees pocket full of
      snipe,
An' me, I go de sam' place, an' I tramp de
      w'ole day long
   An' I 'm only shootin' two or t'ree, Ba
      Cripe!

I start about de sunrise, an' I put out ma
      decoy,
   An' I see Bateese he sneak along de shore,
An' before it 's comin' breakfas', he 's holler
      on hees boy
For carry home two dozen duck or more.

An' I 'm freezin' on de blin'—me—from four
      o'clock to nine
   An' ev'ry duck she 's passin' up so high.
Dere 's blue-bill an' butter-ball, an' red-head,
      de fines' kin'
   An' I might as well go shootin' on de sky.

Don't see de noder feller lak' Bateese was
        lucky man,
    He can ketch de smartes' feesh is never
        sweem,
An' de bird he seldom miss dem, let dem try
        de hard dey can
    W'y de eagle on de mountain can't fly
        away from heem.

But all de bird, an' feesh too, is geev up
        feelin' scare,
    An' de rabbit he can stay at home in bed,
For he feesh an' shoot no longer, ole Jean
        Bateese Belair,
    'Cos he 's dead.

De Bell of Saint Michel

Go 'way, go 'way, don't ring no more, ole
      bell of Saint Michel,
For if you do, I can't stay here, you know dat
      very well,
No matter how I close ma ear, I can't shut
      out de soun',
It rise so high 'bove all de noise of dis beeg
      Yankee town.

An' w'en it ring, I t'ink I feel de cool, cool
      summer breeze
Dat 's blow across Lac Peezagonk, an' play
      among de trees,
Dey 're makin' hay, I know mese'f, can smell
      de pleasant smell
O! how I wish I could be dere today on
      Saint Michel!

It 's fonny t'ing, for me I 'm sure, dat 's
    travel ev'ryw'ere,
How moche I t'ink of long ago w'en I be
    leevin' dere;
I can't 'splain dat at all, at all, mebbe it 's
    naturel,
But I can't help it w'en I hear de bell of
    Saint Michel.

Dere 's plaintee t'ing I don't forget, but I
    remember bes'
De spot I fin' wan day on June de small
    san'piper's nes'
An' dat hole on de reever w'ere I ketch de
    beeg, beeg trout
Was very nearly pull me in before I pull
    heem out.

An' leetle Elodie Leclaire, I wonner if she
    still
Leev jus' sam' place she use to leev on noder
    side de hill.
But s'pose she marry Joe Barbeau, dat 's
    alway hangin' roun'
Since I am lef' ole Saint Michel for work on
    Yankee town

Ah! dere she go, ding dong, ding dong, it's
    back, encore again
An' ole chanson come on ma head of *a la
    claire fontaine,*
I'm not surprise it soun' so sweet, more
    sweeter I can tell
For wit' de song also I hear de bell of
    Saint Michel.

It's very strange about dat bell, go ding
    dong all de w'ile
For when I'm small garcon at school, can't
    hear it half a mile;
But seems more farder I get off from Church
    of Saint Michel,
De more I see de ole vill age an' louder
    soun' de bell.

O! all de monee dat I mak' w'en I be travel
    roun'
Can't kip me long away from home on dis
    beeg Yankee town,
I t'ink I'll settle down again on Parish
    Saint Michel,
An' leev an' die more satisfy so long I hear
    dat bell.

Leetle Lac Grenier

Leetle Lac Grenier, she 's all alone,
Right on de mountain top,
But cloud sweepin' by, will fin' tam' to stop
No matter how quickly he want to go,
So he 'll kiss leetle Grenier down below.

Leetle Lac Grenier, she 's all alone,
Up on de mountain high
But she never feel lonesome, 'cos for w'y?
So soon as de winter was gone away
De bird come an' sing to her ev'ry day.

Leetle Lac Grenier, she 's all alone,
Back on de mountain dere,
But de pine tree an' spruce stan' ev'ryw'ere
Along by de shore, an' mak' her warm
For dey kip off de win' an' de winter storm.

Leetle Lac Grenier, she's all alone,
No broder, no sister near,
But de swallow will fly, an' de beeg moose deer
An' caribou too, will go long way
To drink de sweet water of Lac Grenier.

Leetle Lac Grenier, I see you now,
Onder de roof of spring
Ma canoe's afloat, an' de robin sing,
De lily's beginnin' her summer dress,
An' trout's wakin' up from hees long long res'.

Leetle Lac Grenier, I'm happy now,
Out on de ole canoe,
For I'm all alone, ma chère, wit' you,
An' if only a nice light rod I had
I'd try dat fish near de lily pad!

Leetle Lac Grenier, O! let me go,
Don't spik no more,
For your voice is strong lak' de rapid's roar,
An' you know youse'f I'm too far away,
For visit you now—leetle Lac Grenier!

Index of Titles

Index of First Lines

The Author

William Henry Drummond was born in
Ireland in 1854, and ten years later emigrated
with his parents to Canada, where the family
settled in a suburb of Montreal. Shortly
afterwards, the father, an officer in the Royal
Irish Constabulary, died, and young
Drummond had to leave school and work as
a telegraph operator in order to help his
struggling family. Some time later he re-entered
high school and was able to continue his
education at McGill University and Bishop's
College Medical School where he was
granted his M.D. in 1884, and where he later
became Professor of Medical Jurisprudence.
Thus his career as a family doctor of the old
school began and the knowledge of human
nature which he acquired from his experiences
with the *habitants* of Quebec who were his
patients soon found expression in his dialect
poems.

The honours which his work as doctor, professor, and poet earned for him included a Fellowship in the Royal Society of Canada in 1899, an LL.D. from Toronto University in 1902, and election to the Royal Society of Literature of England. In 1905 he moved to Kerr Lake near Cobalt where he operated the Drummond Mine until his death from cerebral haemorrhage brought on from overwork during a smallpox epidemic in 1907.

His first book, *The Habitant and Other French-Canadian Poems,* with an introduction by Louis Fréchette, appeared in 1897, and was followed by *Phil-o-rum's Canoe and Madeleine Verchères* (1898), *Johnnie Courteau and Other Poems* (1901), *The Voyageur and Other Poems* (1905), and, posthumously, *The Great Fight* (1908), which contains a biographical preface by his wife, May Harvey Drummond. In 1912 his collected *Poetical Works* was published.

THE NEW CANADIAN LIBRARY LIST

n 1. OVER PRAIRIE TRAILS / Frederick Philip Grove
n 2. SUCH IS MY BELOVED / Morley Callaghan
n 3. LITERARY LAPSES / Stephen Leacock
n 4. AS FOR ME AND MY HOUSE / Sinclair Ross
n 5. THE TIN FLUTE / Gabrielle Roy
n 6. THE CLOCKMAKER / Thomas Chandler Haliburton
n 7. THE LAST BARRIER AND OTHER STORIES / Charles G. D. Roberts
n 8. BAROMETER RISING / Hugh MacLennan
n 9. AT THE TIDE'S TURN AND OTHER STORIES / Thomas H. Raddall
n10. ARCADIAN ADVENTURES WITH THE IDLE RICH / Stephen Leacock
n11. HABITANT POEMS / William Henry Drummond
n12. THIRTY ACRES / Ringuet
n13. EARTH AND HIGH HEAVEN / Gwethalyn Graham
n14. THE MAN FROM GLENGARRY / Ralph Connor
n15. SUNSHINE SKETCHES OF A LITTLE TOWN / Stephen Leacock
n16. THE STEPSURE LETTERS / Thomas McCulloch
n17. MORE JOY IN HEAVEN / Morley Callaghan
n18. WILD GEESE / Martha Ostenso
n19. THE MASTER OF THE MILL / Frederick Philip Grove
n20. THE IMPERIALIST / Sara Jeannette Duncan
n21. DELIGHT / Mazo de la Roche
n22. THE SECOND SCROLL / A. M. Klein
n23. THE MOUNTAIN AND THE VALLEY / Ernest Buckler
n24. THE RICH MAN / Henry Kreisel
n25. WHERE NESTS THE WATER HEN / Gabrielle Roy
n26. THE TOWN BELOW / Roger Lemelin
n27. THE HISTORY OF EMILY MONTAGUE / Frances Brooke
n28. MY DISCOVERY OF ENGLAND / Stephen Leacock
n29. SWAMP ANGEL / Ethel Wilson
n30. EACH MAN'S SON / Hugh MacLennan
n31. ROUGHING IT IN THE BUSH / Susanna Moodie
n32. WHITE NARCISSUS / Raymond Knister
n33. THEY SHALL INHERIT THE EARTH / Morley Callaghan
n34. TURVEY / Earle Birney
n35. NONSENSE NOVELS / Stephen Leacock
n36. GRAIN / R. J. C. Stead
n37. LAST OF THE CURLEWS / Fred Bodsworth
n38. THE NYMPH AND THE LAMP / Thomas H. Raddall
n39. JUDITH HEARNE / Brian Moore
n40. THE CASHIER / Gabrielle Roy
n41. UNDER THE RIBS OF DEATH / John Marlyn
n42. WOODSMEN OF THE WEST / M. Allerdale Grainger
n43. MOONBEAMS FROM THE LARGER LUNACY / Stephen Leacock
n44. SARAH BINKS / Paul Hiebert
n45. SON OF A SMALLER HERO / Mordecai Richler
n46. WINTER STUDIES AND SUMMER RAMBLES / Anna Jameson
n47. REMEMBER ME / Edward Meade
n48. FRENZIED FICTION / Stephen Leacock
n49. FRUITS OF THE EARTH / Frederick Philip Grove
n50. SETTLERS OF THE MARSH / Frederick Philip Grove
n51. THE BACKWOODS OF CANADA / Catharine Parr Traill
n52. MUSIC AT THE CLOSE / Edward McCourt
n53. MY REMARKABLE UNCLE / Stephen Leacock